A
SLOW
FUSE

A SLOW FUSE

NEW POEMS

THEODORE WEISS

COLLIER BOOKS
MACMILLAN PUBLISHING COMPANY
NEW YORK

COLLIER MACMILLAN PUBLISHERS
LONDON

Macmillan Publishing Company
866 Third Avenue, New York, N.Y. 10022
Collier Macmillan Canada, Inc.

Library of Congress Cataloging in Publication Data

Weiss, Theodore Russell, 1916–
  A slow fuse.

  I. Title.
PS3545.E4735S55 1984   811'.54   84-12639
ISBN 0-02-071040-2 (pbk.)

10   9   8   7   6   5   4   3   2   1

A Slow Fuse is also published in a hardcover edition
by Macmillan Publishing Company.

Printed in the United States of America

ACKNOWLEDGMENTS

Grateful acknowledgment is made to the editors of the following publications for permission to reprint some of the poems in this book: *The American Poetry Review* for "As If a Rain," "A Slow Fuse," "A Pair of Shoes," "Under the Appearance of . . . ," "A Collaboration," "Sound," "The Hostage," "Looking Back"; *Canto* for "At the Border"; *The Iowa Review* for "Coming Attractions"; *Manhattan Poetry Review* for "Fellow Travelers"; *Mudfish* for "Traveling Third Class"; *The Nation* for "The Jupon"; *New Letters* for "The Readings"; *The New Republic* for "En Route"; *The Ontario Review* for "In Passing," "Living It Up," "In Praise of What Passes," "Word for Word," "A Walk in the Park," "Variations on a Favorite Theme"; *Pivot* for "A Listening Flute"; *Poems for Shakespeare 9* for "Reprise" (now "Every Second Thought"); *Present Tense* for "Making It"; *The Seattle Review* for "One Wet Autumn Afternoon"; *Southwest Review* for "A Living Room"; *TriQuarterly* for "The Here and Now," "A Building," "The Death of Fathers," "Earthrise"; *The View from the Top of the Mountain* for "Mainstay"; *The Yale Review* for "Camel in the Snow," "Piecemeal."

CONTENTS

A
SLOW
FUSE

A LIVING ROOM

for Hannah Arendt and Heinrich Blücher
"The past is never dead, it is not even past."

I

THESE BRITTLE PAGES spread before me,
letter, manuscript, should store
some fragrance, glints long gathering.
Or at least the storm which bodies,
matching, once had set.
                              The breathing,
different, catches: passages, this one,
that, their phrases off pitch, stiff,
seem to be straining to remember.

What a time it is, this time
let out, as though I've jimmied
a closet till now hid
                              (much like
       the closet I found years ago
       behind some beams, a bed, a heavy
       chest of drawers, in an old
       Bath lodging house,
                              which opened
       on, discarded with its century,
       the cornice of a massive building),

free within its atmosphere to be
nothing but itself, attend to nothing
but itself.

II

             There, for a moment,
like some eye considering the view
beneath its lid a world enough,
a living room.
                   And late-noon-silvered
willows which had never made it
into these pages sprinkle twilight
(mountain pines beyond already mining
the harvest moon, a mass of shimmers)
through the room.
                   As through it,

1

sounding out the dark, the char-
plush rustle of a train, its smoke
coiling in the trees. Or rain arrived,
an earlier version, offering glosses.

Still like words worn down, the rain
asserting shapes too distant to remark,
these pages keep their strangeness.

Possibly out of the dust collecting
a later time will fathom them.
By then the people somewhere inside
may, returning, look to one out here.

III

One out here?
          A grey December Princeton
morning lours like a giant shadow
that a snow, fast approaching, casts,
a train puffing along, and we lost
in it, lost inside its cloud of smoke.

Despite their bulk, in faded summer-
gaudy jackets even my stoutest volumes
flitter, while the Persian reproduction
on the wall, its light-clad figures
ruffled, flaps before the icy blasts.

And I, pulling out a plain brown
envelope stuffed through the mail-slot,
read the name scribbled in the upper
lefthand corner,
          name of her I saw
just yesterday at a popular Manhattan
memorial chapel, in a narrow plain
brown wooden box filling the very spot
her husband filled five years before
when she we'd thought so self-possessed
had riveted her gaze fast to his face.

Her packet's note transfixes me:

    "Such a terrible long time since I
    last saw you and talked with you.

2

Don't you ever come to New York?
I'm getting less and less willing
to move. . . . take this as an excuse
to call me."

IV

Hannah, young vibrant muse
to Heidegger, Jaspers' spiritual daughter,
German confidante and English of Jarrell,
Auden's final choice for a companion
("I came back to New York only because
of you."), Heinrich's chief, abiding lover,
gruff, imperious,
                              thick smoky wreaths
ubiquitous around her blurted words,
now in the living room of their apart-
ment looking out upon the easygoing
Hudson, noon compiling ripples—
                                                    quivered
like her city's spires, ancient cities
she, loving, had to leave—which echo
squealing cars and roaring buses, loose
on Riverside Drive, the last time I see her
(Heinrich, "alive in every corner and at
every moment," hovering between us) alive,

and she, finally deciding what
I long have hoped for: "Heinrich's lectures"—
the main reason for our months on months
of meeting, but foiled in each attempt
("Why it's as if that humpback imp, mischief
its delight, never lost sight of us!")—
      "I alone must shape for publication,"

bustling over me, a proper Jewish mother,
feeds me chicken soup with dumplings!

V

Midweek and Heinrich knocking at my door:
      "I want your book of poems at once.
      Tomorrow I am to see a publisher."
He brooking no demur, my protesting
it not finished, off it goes with him.

3

That Friday in New York to teach
the course that Heinrich had arranged
("You are too much a stick in the mud
in Bard."), before our classes as he
nears, I see that something's happened.

    "Ted, I don't know how to tell you
    this. But when I got to New York,
    my cab dashing off, your book was gone.
    Since then and with the police I have
    been looking for it everywhere."

Though, beyond some printed poems
and earlier drafts, nothing remains, I,
remarking his distress, must comfort him.
The Scarlet Letter I uncover to my class
flares out livid as it's ever been.

Should I blame him, who fled the Nazis
over several countries, for enabling
through solicitude that manuscript
to join those countless other works
destroyed?
        Who then deserves my rancor?

VI
"You don't know me?
O look and see.
This crookback's my
identity.

An elf from tales
of Germany,
I've popped into
the USA.

Of your bad luck
the guardian,
if your pot breaks
by me it's done.

A miser hooked
on misery,
when trouble strikes
and someone wails,

4

I am most gay,
as now when you,
too busy, fail
to notice me.

So I bestow
my dear regards.
Account your loss
my calling card."

Ah well, bowed down before this blow,
must I not also pray for that ingenious
hail-fellow?
Who else, by cursing,
so successfully prevails on me
to trim my lines for such emergencies
and then in turn cooks up emergencies
(O ironies!) quite the reverse,

VII

as Hannah's note, continuing, reveals:

"Today going through Heinrich's papers
I found a folder with poems from you.
I hope to God you have copies.
Anyway, I'm sending it back to you
in case anything in your files
is missing.

Warm regards.

Yours,
Hannah."

Missing? Here and now, nearly two
decades later, that manuscript,
my book-to-be, *Outlanders*, somewhere
buried among Heinrich's papers, spread
before me!
Nothing other than the brief
confusion rushing about from train
to taxi with a pile of books and papers,
the crookback happily helping, can produce.
Though Heinrich's scorn for our spawning
volumes might have also been at work.

An autodidact he, admiring the pariah,
any man free-standing, that naked flute-
player, lounging buoyant, while she pipes
a meditative tune, upon her stele
as upon the Greek postcard he sent us.

Uneasy, torn between German and English,
he, like Lao-tse at the border, customs
fronting, would declare but one short
statement which, transparent, potent,
as a water drop, must change the world.

Small wonder writing comes so hard.

VIII

Instead Heinrich of the high places,
dapper past hope or fear and gone past
expectations of others, so accepting,
open to—at first this broad camaraderie
offended me—each one, yet hoping still,
devoted like Hannah to community,
the polis,
            Heinrich with his thin cigars,
his thick Berliner accent, deep down
grumbles, flash-eyed shoutings, spouting
like Vesuvius in their old world living
room amid the clash of amiable minds,

arguing, not less than with his friends
and Hannah's, with their dearest intimates,
Homer, Plato, Nietzsche, Kafka, Faulkner,
as though, everlasting in the flesh,
their minds still musing and through him
and her still making up their minds,

in the arrows he lets loose, no matter
what extremity may corner him, insouciant
since never losing sight of the bull's eye
(he, fancying himself a military expert—
once recruited by the Kaiser's army,
had he not learned to elude the Nazis?—
his inspired, dashing troops deployed,
resorts to rashest sallies and ambushes,
raids),

addresses each Bard freshman class
as though the elders, august senators,
of Athens were assembled before him:

IX

"An artist never raises the question
directly since he cannot doubt—
as a pregnant woman, under normal
circumstances, scarcely doubts—
the value of life.
                    Yet he alone
lives this question permanently,
his whole work one emphatic answer.
The artist's impulse springs from the
initial shock that meaninglessness
is possible at all, let alone
boredom and banality;
                        this shock
provokes an immediate transcending
action, which, contradicting
the question itself, by Beauty's aura
again and again assures the artist
and the beholder that, awaiting one
bold enough to wake it, meaning exists
everywhere."
              Several students, bemused,
then gaping, promptly slump into sleep;
others stare, incredulous at what
their ears are taking in; but a few,
like new buds thirsting, guzzle it
while Socrates, a fulltime talker also
impatient of pale writing, once more,
bantering his distraught companions,
nonchalantly quaffs the bitter cup.

    "My friends, promise me, whatever happens,
    you will not contrive, and least of all
    with drugs, to rob me of my death."

(Aging, his crack troops, scattered
far afield in wind and snow, contend
with tough guerrilla bands more and more
elusive, daring.
                  To retrieve these forces

from remote, harsh desert lands exacts
an always greater effort. And returning,
exhaustion weighs on them, the strain
of fending off a growing enemy.)

X

                     But I,
hearing from Hannah and Heinrich together,
as if a stormy spell may still be coiling
through the pages of my manuscript,
shove it into a crowded drawer.

As much dare look at that crookback
chortling here, at Heinrich's lectures
stowed away on some secluded shelf.

Let them declare, like lidded lavender
the names still green and branching out
in memory, the meaning everywhere!

XI

All parts of the Olympic games,
the gods bent over, eagerly regarding?

Hannah agrees:

> "One goes there for fame; another,
> for trade. But the best ones sit there
> in the amphitheater just to look.
> Only such can get the gist out of it.
>
> So, while some are chiefly interested
> in doing, I am not. Looking, you see,
> is what I am after. I can very well
> live without doing anything. Therefore,
> I get less and less willing to move.
>
> You think me passive? I, by nature,
> am not an actor. A pariah from the start,
> a woman and a Jew, thought, not doing,
> I much preferred.
>   And even when Heinrich
> (after Hitler!) beat me over the head
> with a hammer, waking me to the urgent,

lesser, murderous realities, I still
had this advantage: to look at the world
from the outside.
            And now, if I intend
to think, I must withdraw. After hard,
long years, the world our passionate care,
have I, to shun the they, their mere talk,
their trivialities, washed over every-
thing, not won the right to such retreat?

A bearing out this thinking is, a blessed
keeping which action itself can never realize.

Sitting here intent, speeding past
all measurement, the way that aspen leaves
sail off at any breeze, is travel enough.

Forgive me, but a little boredom is
quite healthy. And, so long as it is not
allowed to overwhelm our appetite
for greatness, some commonplace as well.

More than enough I've traveled,
the blurred, lurching ships and trains,
the hissing waves, the belching smoke,
the jammed-up boxcar we just missed
turning soon enough into that smoke-
bound car nothing stops, nobody misses.

Pondering the world, its rush of strange
events, mishaps, yes, even monstrosities,
which, free as they are, unpredictable,
our story-telling proves inevitable,
I cannot live without trying every day
to understand—and never, up and down
the slippery stairs, a bannister to lean
on—the wonder of their being, meaning.

Poetry, yours, is it so different?

Thinking, freed of physical obstacles,
for me amounts to sheer activity.
In the older Cato's words, 'When I do
nothing I am most active, and when I'm
by myself, I am the least alone.'

9

The moment you cannot sit still,
cannot admit plurality, the endless
dialogue between yourself and you,
contending with the world, you surely
stumble over your own feet. As Plato
said, 'Your body always wants to be
taken care of and to hell with it!' "

XII

And yet are we not after pleasure,
the passions, even the most painful,
pouring forth their rhapsodies as they
erupt in and through the bodied mind
out of collision with the world, lust
in the best of us for pleasure so vast
it seeks whatever excess, outrage
earth can muster?
                    Needs it—as some
plants require fiercest storms to tear
away their outer husks—and needs
to praise, praise which, pitting itself
against the worst, sucks honey strength
out of the wound that tales be told,
songs sung, praise.

XIII

                    August blazing,
I spend the day with Hannah and Heinrich
in Palenville. This summer once again
they occupy a little, box-like cottage
to escape the city's jungle squalor and,
among the Catskills, rugged path and wake
of a volcano—
                    climbing them, the jolt
of every step on rock throughout the body,
one can feel that first volcano still,
its aspiration, as it hurled itself,
voluminous fire, headlong in the heavens—

to recover from the year's thick rigors
as from our storm-beleagured epoch,
though their windows show a village
sprawled in shacks and dumps, garages,

which confirms that they, adjusting old
familiar terrors to the foreign new
as to abasements opening on depths
still able to surprise, are still adrift
aboard the ship set sail with crew—
its passengers stroll into view—unseen,
its orders and its destination sealed.

XIV

Inevitably talk of poetry prevails.
Another visitor, a charter member
of their tribe, hand to her brow
as if to help her understand, inquires:

"Pray tell, how do you Americans manage?
Never to learn by heart beloved poems
for the dark and lonely times! Who are
your companions then?"
                                            And as I hunch
forward in the simple living room
between Hannah and Heinrich, suddenly
a unison, they chant; their phrases,
soaring
            ("Da stieg ein Baum. O reine
            Übersteigung!"),
                                    smitten like their con-
concentrated glances by the molten sun
descending, glitter.
                            I am caught
up in the empyrean middle—a capacious
temple, perched as on a sky-capped summit,
building of that terrible, blithe marble,
only stone to last in being lava still
like bristling stars, the stately breath—
of the first of *Die Sonette an Orpheus.*

There, for a moment, in that double
sibilance, and flared as by a burning-
glass, the paired-off animals draw near,
their stir, their roars, now stilled,
all ears to learn their private names,
I too—the moon already, famous with
the wind-strummed pines, allotting light—
engrossed among these numberless regards.

11

XV

More than ten years past, having come
this far in the poem, I pause, dig out
the manuscript and, riffling through,
dare look at its like-coffin-browning
pages.
      Some of the poems differ
from my final versions; others take
me, strangers, by surprise, yet promptly
for their stiff-locked cadence spring
to mind.
      At once I'm in a living
room, its windows flung wide open
to the sky, as if, someone unfolding
a letter—
      pressed inside its leaves
a tiny, faded flower, mountain laurel,
what is left of one particular morning—
morning, atop this autumn afternoon,
is blazoning forth;
      gusts rousing
out of trees and braided with day's ric-
ochet from mountains hulked behind,
a couple dally, once more fledglings
nestled like the larks that towered round
them, rue-and-laurel-interwoven wreath.

XVI

And I not looking back, yet looking,
feeling like an ore long buried struck
or like a river as it, riding, deepens
for its travels down inside a cavern
out to sea,
      these two (have they not
waited all this time ahead of me?) break,
sparkling, forth upon the blood's whole-
hearted tide out on this stream of notes,
a storming, my breath dares to flourish
in the dark.
      This way they look to me . . .

IN PASSING

As you speed by, a boy
waving, some cows at munching,
horses glossy for the double light—
your eyelashes' liquid blinking
swifter than thought brushing
them down—
                    in one lifetime
how many sights can you expect
to spend more than a quick glance
on? Cattails wagging, dandelions,
this rushing, forsaken field.

Or a short delay for signals
at a crossroads, and the vista
down the enfilading maples, each
thickened with shade, one lopsided
shack, a man in khaki sprawled
on a bench, a dog,
                        chickens,
kids tumbled round in the dirt.
You have lived long enough to know
you must not loiter. If you did
dust would spread,
                        the curse
of habit, eye its own grim mote.
These junked cars quarry lightning
from the setting sun, astonished
by the dents into a momentary
temple
            beggars the opulence
of Solomon. Surpassing like one
prophet's shortlived Pisgah sights,
he thereby spared that maelstrom,
jammed-up sandstorms, named
Jerusalem.
                Each scene nothing
better than a station to pause in
before resuming speed?
                                Train
rushed along, huge battering ball,
you easily shuck the world, vaguer
than wrecks dumping behind.

13

Still
they work to get you through,
momentum of a sort,
               a gasoline,
that field sufficient for a flight
of crows, the wind swinging in
a tree, a brook looked out,
emphatic inquiries.
               Indeed,
though it's not Delphi, no site
outstanding in its cliffs, ravines,
events which centuries ago had
carved it out, what it has
to do it does.
               Our world's
so cupboard-crammed we've little
need to hoard or dally. Let things
go their separate ways, a will
at work unlimited by ours.

A LISTENING FLUTE

(as if a music overheard)

LATE JANUARY, yet the sun
piles up, great willowy bales,
and, as if lit from within, haloes
every thing.
   The days,
aeons upon aeons of, under-
ground long drowsing, this day
piles up in the brain,
      a hive
where nectar is distilling.
The body sheathes it too,
highway for its trafficking
delight:
   though body sits,
a centaur stabled in its chair,
it dreams out giant voyages,
exotic harbors,
     cities old
and new somewhere hunched in it,
these churning through its sleep
like that squat,
    arthritic crab-
apple, with its secret panic
leaves and fruits:
     a fury
that embraces biting gales,
for it still hoards the fire
strokes by which it was first
hammered out.
    Somewhere in me,
past the storms still brooding,
flexing sinews in their wind
and sleet,
    yet through them,
something made of bone, a flute—
around it a vast desert spread,
its rats and stony newts scuttled
along as they beat out
      its tune,
which, blowing, interwoven with

the flame, should illuminate
the cave—
      is listening for music
(listening itself a music), massive
since more lightsome than an ear
can bear.

TRAVELING THIRD CLASS

AT TIMES you wonder what it's like
wandering about in someone else's head.
Like suddenly being dropped in sleep
into a foreign country, its speech
almost familiar,
      but slipping away
the streets, the buildings, not entirely
strange and yet arranged in patterns
that escape you.
      As a swallow might dip
then sweep your image like a twig
into the sky, a hovering.
      Or zipped past
you on an autumn stroll, each leaf
a sunset echoing late day, an eye, casual
from a bus, with one blink thrusts you
into a melee, a wild sea-like thrashing
you, instantly become a perfect stranger
to yourself, can never navigate alone.

Else plunged into the rapture
of icy water with a bluefish you hold
a second on your quivering line, and both
united in that tussle as it, darted away,
for very eagerness takes bait and you
to green-dark recesses only coral-
fathomed.
      Even more amazing, sunk
into the scattered thoughts of someone
dying and, dirt drowning you, emptied out
into a worm's mouth, your jumbled cells
now free in water taproots and someone

16

else—a pike, a dusk-brave muskrat—
drink.
            And so you take yourself
from every hand, this apple, plumped
with people rampant in its tangy flesh,
news of yourself about to be, the latest
leaves a kind of visa, travel also,
on their winter-driven maple,
                              travel
wolves somewhere are sponsoring, the herd
of deer sped farthest in their ravening.

CAMEL IN THE SNOW

PROFESSIONALS of snow,
the Eskimos mint many terms off it:
snow-at-sunset, snow-inside-an-igloo,
snow-tears-turn-to-icicles, a snow-
a-bear-is-tracking, snow-blood-
splatters.
            And in Arabic also
words amounting to five-thousand-
seven-hundred-and-eighty-four steam
from the camel.
            As though those
and thousands crowding thousands more,
coupling night and day, could tell
the whole story!
            As though,
given helpmate camel and the snow,
constants through the hurlyburly
of a life, one or the other does not
become—each word precisely spoked
from it—the axis for whatever happens.

You and I have lived together
over forty years, traveled through
some twenty countries. Well, are you,
the habits, whims, minute details of,
not my weather, for one happy spell
balm jasmine breathes, the next
wind-sinewed snow?

                                  The wide world
desert at an instant turned into one
baffling sand-storm, a gaunt camel
rides me madly through;
                        nomadic,
driven by the windy heat, it glides
into another blinding blast, snow,
wildly falling, covering all, a hump
among unmoving humps.
                                  That camel,
thick or thin, water sloshing in it,
clumps along, with days and nights,
a drove of vultures, sheep and drivers,
jeweled oases, fat flakes whirling
off its gallop.
                        Meantime, I, tossed
hither, yon, try reining it with words
in mighty swarms, since like the Eskimo
I know no single term redoubtable enough
for anything this living-changeable,
this mixed up with our lives, as (camel
also) snow.

LIVING IT UP

"POETRY? Too much for me,"
she frowned. "Exaggerated as it is,
contrived, one can't trust it:

all those highfalutin
moods the poet means to cash
in on, especially as he lacks them.

As for feelings he does
have, deceit so long his way,
straining to make more of himself

than he is, they finally,
no less than those first, fall in
with fancy feigning."
                              These words
of hers have gone on haunting;
and never more
                    than now
they tantalize, for she sends
messages to her friend, my sister-

in-law, calm, rational,
self-mocking letters, from an
institution they committed her to,

having caught her living
it up, buying things, cashing
checks for funds she did not have.

PIECEMEAL

A JAGGED CRY, breaking
out, and breaking into you
as through this pre-dawn sky,
plucks you out of sleep.

Finch it may be, lark,
but abrupt as though it too
erupts from the bird's dream,
in a wilful flourishing

surprises it. Yet you,
groping for hands (your own?),
for limbs, a mind, fall back
mid-operation, scraps

strewn on a white sheet.
And you would submit to being,
like some backwater, drowse-
prone hamlet, trampled

by invading troops
that pillage as they rape,
then spread big fire, killings
by the legion, slashing dark.

But day's first azure
combers washing over, bit
by bit you stir, as if, hands
rummaging in you, remote

messages like minerals
deep in the earth, the nuggets
of the marigolds about to be,
tap through. Soon, bones

assembled, that body
by you fitting you, so fitting
you together, and the mouth
apt beyond that deep-sea-

diving, heart coerced
with its marauding dreams,
exultant in their own distress,
into its daytime hiding

place, you surface,
the scattered pieces fused
out of the mists. Dawn, falcon-
wise, tugs at your wrist.

THE JUPON

OVER the official luncheon
she remembers, and through the dust-
specked glasses her eyes sparkle, as if
those noble lives, light welled from them,
focus there.
      Old Canterbury sleeping
now, that courtly couple side by side,
except when visitors like her would stir
retainers, hounds, the wars, the revelries
they swept round them, a world akin
to far-flung birds, boughs, fountains
spun into a tapestry encompassing
a lady and her love.
      But a jupon
it is catches in the speaker's throat,
that pied surcoat the Black Prince wore,
donned for special occasions only, neatly
mended through the centuries by nuns
until, she is convinced, no single snip
of the original remains. And yet, she says,
it is most beautiful.
      "Why," you offer,
"just like us: every stitch of the old Adam
gone, only the gusto of that itch prevails
that flung him out beyond the fiery gates,
follies evergreen he'd thereafter prove
to the last ditch—and through our persons—
perfect gardener to.

Does not a slip
of that parent garden, twining itself,
throughout the maze a thread unbreakable
for all the Fall and its long lineage,
in every leaf, still urgently festoon
fruits of its nature? But the blood drawn
to stain them properly!
                                        Should you care
to examine us more closely you would see—
whatever time's repeated tailorings,
one motley patch the cloth, each epoch out
to make its mark—the first design shine
through, no doubt defined more sharply
than when brandnew."

AT THE BORDER

AND WHEN YOU TRY, your body taut,
to make your way in French, Italian,
not to mention tongues we hardly know,
are we not both—you first, I shuffled
after you—entranced?
                              As though,
stepped into an exotic if insistent
past, you venture to recall old things,
its basic elements.
                              And I, loving
that certain sense of you poured in
upon your words, the English you apply
to everything, fix eyes, fix ears,
on you:
              a traffic of far different
worlds swirled round, advancing
as within a maze, yet moving timely
to its complex dance, you fluster me.

(For who's to say what stowaways,
what drugs, forbidden books and bugs,
what schemes pumped on our private air
to prosper, here get smuggled in?)

Still, though I clutch your hand
in fear that you, grown more assured,
might suddenly disappear, I understand
these languages, not you, are being
moved into.
                    A harvest moon, should
it not, retorting, influence the sun,
as a translation in some lesser tongue
thereafter casts increasing shadows
on and through its original?
                                          But
squeezed, poor rattlesome, between,
dour earth the sun and moon conspire
to expose, I,
                    even as I, squinting
and revising, strain to master both,
twice at least turned out (O vertigo!),
a babble, at their border flap about.

23

A BUILDING

to house
these maddened times, these squalid,
brawling lives? (Happily wasps
are sizzling, total war
over a muddy pool.)
 Nearby
the sea sprawls, an incurable
complaint. Worse than gypsies we,
our path rutted far past recognition,
rove about,
 yet like sands
tumbled, by the breezes tossing
and the sea, namelessly in one place:
rubble we pass, aimless suburbs,
ever the same.
 Only a wren,
building its nest in our runted
catalpa tree, savors the ensolacings
of its trill (boughs once blew,
wilful leaves;
 Brother Wood,
walking by man's side, gave fish,
fruit, songs: each season in its turn,
each day, for the new youth won
to explore itself,
 friskier).
But who can long abide in flaws
of man-made weather . . . one sluggish
August day, the heat like a mob
grown ugly,
 by the Hudson's
east bank an old cow (its trail
founded this city) bloated with many
days' death; stench proclaimed
the fury of devotion.
 Prodded
the belly, seething rose: a snarl
of eels dragged forth from the river
up the steep, miry path, to prop
the love-churned walls.

AS IF A RAIN

As IF a rain could love
to ramble through our trees
while rambling slowly, slowly
through itself, recalling
as it murmurs spots it's been
to, sundry things it's seen,

reflected in it, grasses,
bird calls echoed distantly,
sighs, naked, of young lovers,
and the deer that, soaking,
lapped at it until sun sucked
it into cloud-besotted sky,

but not before the blood,
the rot and filth it entered,
blinking nothing, as it footed
through the dark, the thicket
cries and mottled corpses,
cheek by jowl with violets,

assorted rowdy scents,
let loose from it as from
each leaf and bush, instant
to its touch, I love to ramble
through the secret grove
your body is,
         to dawdle
in its mazy byways, basking
in the fragrant warmth the sun
has gathered there, of light
and shadow, as they mate,
the intricacies,
         that crowd
of hands applauding you and me,
like ripened pippins pelting
us from every side, a wind-
fall the considerate rain
of you surprises

out of me,
breeding a dance so confident
it, leisurely invading, gambols
through our limbs—the leaves
a kind of madcap clapping—
as among itself.

A SLOW FUSE

SEVENTY years later
your father, sitting at your table
over wine he savors, last rays mellow-
ing in it, recalls his favorite aunt,
Rifka.
      "Just naming her shoots
rifles off again inside the morning
square, rifles she aimed into the air
for certain customers, the pigeons
erupting."
      Handsome, clever,
but with little actual schooling,
she, a Jewess, kept a shop in Moscow
stocking horse- and battle-gear,
busy all day long.
      The powders,
braided with his laboring breath,
still prickle inside his nostrils;
like the wayward flickers cast
by lazily swimming,
      naked limbs,
leathers, buckles, polishes gleam;
and the oats banked in their bins,
heavy August winds drowsed in them,
at one glance, a single sniffing,
flare;
      the harnesses and bells,
by gas-light starred, send out appeals,
while sleighs go at advancing rates
of winter.
      He smitten with it all,
like those officers of the Czar
who, admiring her wit, her ardent
gaiety, forever jammed the shop.

"Even the city's metropolitan,
young despite his full, black robes,
enjoyed dropping in on her, his jagged,
bushy beard awag with chat.
      One balmy
summer evening, I remember, the three
of us, jokes brimming over like this
wine, relaxed in her snug flat.

The next morning at breakfast,
talk going on as if it never stopped"—
he, a startled look lit on his face,
breaking in upon himself, exclaims,
the pigeons crackling through the air—
"My God, he spent the night with her!"

He, sipping the last drop, sits
back, as much as he's amazed amused
to see this special virtue of old age,
the oats ripening only in slow time.

A PAIR OF SHOES

THIS YOU WERE SURE, whatever happened,
you'd remember, long as any thought
stuck in your head.
          After a bitter
winter, when you and your family had
to eat weeds, bark, scraps of leather,
and it seemed certain the caked ice
would last forever,
          the first lull came
drifting over. And then, more sudden
than the dusk invading, a tattered army,
raping, looting, killed all the others,
burned down the huts, and disappeared
before the smoke could scatter.
          This
you were sure you'd remember, the blood
of your mother soaked in her blouse.

That was how many epochs, how many
countries, earthquakes, holocausts ago?
And oceans washing through, the cloudy
dreams, how many furnished rooms, a rusty
stain on them from how many people?

Now you are old and bent over, old
and bent to this spot called New York.
And crossing the street, only one thing
matters—see the wide shadow it casts!—
to keep these broken, laceless shoes,
three sizes too big, from falling off.

Beside such chore, your left foot
slowly, slowly sliding after the other,
what a far off, foolish tale that memory.
Let those sporting a polished pair
which fit indulge themselves.
          Crossing
this street, the weight of you collected,
the old blood shuffles through your veins,
too busy to remember.

UNDER THE APPEARANCE OF . . .

REALITY of a basic kind,
even as it is local and therefore
seemingly commonplace, you begin to think,
underlies extraordinary appearances.

This curator, stumbling on
a painting he recognizes a Vermeer,
but knowing he cannot export it as it is,
orders a copy of some lesser work

slapped across the original.
And so he smuggles it out. At home
the restorer writes to him, "I've removed
the fake (whoever it is) and the fake

Vermeer under it. What shall
I do with the wretched portrait remaining
of the young Mussolini?" So, you recall,
Vermeer copies in the thirties duped

the experts. But now we see,
as people of that period could not,
that all the faces looked like Greta Garbo.
In that sense those copies were not

in any way fake but faithful,
as Vermeer had been, to their own
time and place and to the special face
their time believed the lasting loveliness.

So the copies of 13th century
Gothic wall-paintings, hailed as authentic
masterpieces, justly so, for they were
more like Gothic wall-paintings

than Gothic paintings themselves:
the forger painted what we saw—our Gothic—
in the originals, painted it directly
without a blurring from the past.

ONE WET AUTUMN AFTERNOON

The rain a hovering?
Gnats in a net they spin,
silver needles loosely knitting,
spooks on speedy stilts.

But it comes to more
than that. It can be over-
heard in the tones those leaves
respond with, variously

pitched oak, chestnut,
sycamore. The alders rasp,
engrossed. Birds also grow more
watery. And the waiter,

wiping table-tops,
adroit if submarine, flips
his napkin in what seems a tide
of well-schooled swipes.

Inside this tidying
relations slither about.
Hard as he tries, the young man
cannot keep his thoughts

on the woman sitting
across from him. Afloat he
feels among this crystal fracas,
bickering in the eaves,

and on the roof debate
which babbles for the over-
whelming much it strives to say.
The chandeliers repeating

rain into a fixture,
each pane looks a crybaby.
And four slouching gamblers see
the cards slip through

their fingers. He
puddle-like content to be
so licked at, prickled, entered,
leaping to each drop,

this way aggrandized,
as he hears the water wash
its hands of the whole business,
sodden down to nothing.

THE IMPERIOUS

(after Robert Graves)

SO YOU, imperious enough, revenging
yourself upon that schoolboy Latin
shoved down your throat, made all
those bloody Roman emperors worse
even than they were.
                         Not that they
needed your skills, the good will
of your anger.
                    Still, omnivorous
for the raw stuff of living, no less
the ultimate, outrageous, ruffian fame,
they might have felt some gratitude
for the homage that your rancor's
largess, so imaginative, bestowed.

After all, one's name mumbled,
scattered into stumbling syllables
as if their legions had been routed,
even by some rheumy gaffer, crouching
at a dwindled fire, must be better
than nothing, one last fly stuttering
away tag-ends of a savage summer.

The time come for your dying,
there, just before it, hard pressed
on you, those skirmishes all over
again, matted in rat-infested mud,
and gaspings for the gas, shells
lobbed whizzing overhead, thrilling
more than ever,
                    in their haphazard,
bedded postures the corpses nonchalant,
and, calling on you, your own killed,
closer—clammy sweat and reeking
wounds—than any of your many lovers.

Who's to say you, like that fly
luxuriating buried in a rotting peach,
did not fumble with your last breath
for that ultimate enjoyment, a morsel
belched up on your tongue, a Roman
plump, imperial word.

FELLOW TRAVELERS

A Blue Light

(grief is speaking)

BUT I INSIST you take me
seriously; if you set out
to humor me so as to put me
in my place, a minor part
of some grand scheme, how can
I do what I am meant to,

                bring
it all together, this winter,
friezes, freakish sculpture,
trees bare sticks clacking
like doors of abandoned barns,
a stark light, racked over all,
my gaze?

        At that each thing
promptly falls into place,
the air itself an edgy thing,
with the wind a wing frozen
in it from its own fanning,

just the way your childhood
Nutzy Henry, sudden at any
window, was, for what he might
irrevocably do, a face freezing
not only you, the other kids,
but mothers too.

           My features
no less frightening and yet
invisible—no creaky, buzzard-
flailing out of bony wings—
spread evenly

               over everything
a blue stark light, a hunger
proud nothing can satisfy,
I also do my work through you.
Never ask whose laughter
or whose scheming interests
I look after.

        But know,
so seriously I take you, take
what between us we are up to,

I promise never to humor you.
Not even though this blue light
look a mocking laughter to you.

The Proof

WAS IT all put on then,
little, vigorous man, obsessed
by a longing for the good—so torn
between admired order and the rages
stormed from you, reason's storms—
to try you, the last precious drop
wrung out of you?
                    You thundering
away at your all-day Sunday piano,
an indomitable faith pounding
in those irresistible mistakes,

as if, chopping your way,
great trees dropping left and right,
through an endless forest, at last
it must give way
                    to golden keys
unlocking an iron-rusty gate
before a square filled with smiling
presences, embodied host of music,

else engaged in fervid arguments—
long hours you plied the Bible
for damning proof—with preachers,
reinforcements, jokes you hoarded,
stories crowding stories,
                    laughter
pouring like a sunlit, nonstop
torrent, like the tub of scalding,
soapy water that your wife dumped
into the snow-encrusted day.

All put on to prove the justice
of this prison world, its hungers
good, its terrors, even the way
you could not do what you thought
you ought to, thought you had to
to survive?

With every wretched
rapture, winsome torture, showered
on you, never any moment ignored,
you clung fast for dear life.

In your capacity the gods,
berserk with greediest delight,
proved at their best.
                    This morning
stretched before you, one more—
the last?—ice-breathing day,
to test your will's resiliency,
as you carefully peel, then bite
into this bitter fruit, a precious
drop wrung out of you, that taste
the gods cannot enjoy alone.

The Place of Laughter

IN SOME COUNTRIES laughter is
hardly allowed, a luxury, a kind
of sin, belonging to the mindless
or the mad.
              So for one poet
"the man who laughs/Has simply
not yet heard the terrible news."
In other countries
                    it exists
almost apart from circumstances,
fruit without a tree, laughter
at—if not
              out of—extremities.
However, in the villages of India,
at least as you observed them,
if the people
              survive at all
they are a joy to watch, polished
by hard times, famine, plagues
trying all their strength,
                    women,
bundles on their heads like crowns,
erectly walking, with a laughter
rarely heard

but acknowledged
through their bodies' movements
and their glances soft if piercing,
the way trees stand,
      welcoming
winter, easing sun-stricken summer
with leaves that seem to listen
as they wave,
      shadowy laughter.
Or that little flower breaking out
from a seed that's had to push
its way through rock.

IN PRAISE OF WHAT PASSES

AGAIN they are tying knots,
elegant love-knots, into the air
with Mozart so that he, humming,
saunters in as though he's never
left and means to stay forever.

The thousandth time you feel
at home and yet for the very ease
of it a little strange as well.
So you lean upon his hungers,
desperations,
           pauper's death,
the nameless grave which will not
melt, not yet—for all his melodies'
dissolvents—the huge stone marker
they failed to settle
           over it.
Earth, disturbed or not, matters
in transit. For you should realize
that you, though you sit still,
are bound,
           like these purple
Siamese African violets appearing
just as you look up, to take a road
you've no awareness of; nor will
you think,
           arriving at the end
of it, the place so very different.
The ingredients, however blended—
the cook that moment comes to
matters—are already here.
           The black
crisp phrase in this brief sequence
you agree to see as a shade, ajar,
depths populating depths inside
(a room maybe,
           sighs issuing,
a woman about to lean out, star-
glittered air surrounding her), takes
no more faith than day or darkness
and the gift
           of instantaneous sight
you accept from either.

EN ROUTE

THINGS we, sinking
in an anytime mid-gloom,
cling to which might pluck us
out of this mess, at least bring
it into momentary focus—no wonder
they grow wonderful,
                              perched
seven stories up in this study
of a spacious New York apartment,
the rooms, every one, cosily lined
with ceiling-high shelves, books
behind books, art-books, records,
paintings, caved as at Lascaux,

the mousy little cat, a thing
of springs, hurtled across the bed-
room, next the study, its mother,
prickly, skittish, hid behind some
topmost, dusty volume,
                              this day
meantime glum enough, the day
before Christmas, at the Riverside,
buses soughing by, the buildings
which glittered Byzantine last night
like Christmas itself, this morning
fuzzy cut-outs of smutched mist,
risen from the river,
                              sitting
at my friend's desk, drawers
no doubt littered with postcards,
letters, bills like crumpled sails
of voyages long over, many a flight
if mainly to his much loved Italy,

and even as we contemplate,
fast coming on, our trip to the Far
East, about to scurry down on us
the teeming Bangkok, Taipei, Tokyo
hordes,
             he this very moment in Rome
sightseeing with Kathleen or maybe,
as in my revery, floating along

on a gondola in Venice, its waves
blown, Byzantine, into shapes
mercurial as their capered colors,

while, for wind's incessant blasts,
our world's become a giant ice-cube,
this metropolis, hunched, one frozen
rock-grey fish,
                    the moon hoar too,
in the stories just above each roof
a cavern crystalline with heroes,
gods and angels, sealed like flies,

inside their wings less gossamer
than you, gliding in the next room
on your violin, good as any gondola
for taking breakers of Monteverdi
to transform this day's stark waters
(how they stream along your notes!),

I clinging to things not my own:
your schooled flotilla, riding high;
this inkwell, all the sighs in it,
the nereids, a once stormy deity,
mostly dried; this bottle of glue,
stuck fast to itself; that jar
of pencils stacked like tiny spears;
and the typewriter with its tiers
on tiers of a population waiting—
then it weeps, cheers, boos—to be
manipulated,
                    able to compose
who knows what score of lightning
phrases, able at once to stab
us into wounds we'd rather keep
concealed, yet thereby sooth them
with the precious balm of something
discovered, something almost
understood.
                    Through plants I squint
out the window, hoping the day,
like the bottle's glue, your notes
entwined, these words, will hold
at least itself together

                              and say
out of the murmurous, daylong surf-
ing buses, trucks, swirled cars
that it, not less than the phone
humming on this desk, contains
assorted messages can find me
out in an instant, targeted
by any cry or cat-quick music,
with a homesick grief, a fiercely
fondling, homecome laughter.
                              O
must disconsolateness, this feeling
unmade up like a many-times-slept-
in bed, this clutter as of leaves
grounded, everywhere a bitten grey,
fit and fit and fit me?

THE HERE AND NOW

for Yehuda Amichai

THOUGH YOU LIVE in a little country,
crammed and crisscrossed with debris,
the past oppressive many times over—
where you buy your grapes David, pausing,
eyes a fiery dark girl, a lusty song
riding his breath, the old dance urgent
at his body; where you buy your bread
Christ, stumbling, stoops to heavy lumber—
you insist on your own loves and griefs,
on living your own life.
                                    So you love
this city, but mainly as it goes on
living its own life, across its roofs
the lines flapping, not gaudy banners,
but sheets and diapers, pants and slips,
at it rehearsing private pleasures.

And though you know you cannot win,
you play the game with all the skill
and love that you can muster, hoping
to keep it, keep it going, whatever
the fierceness in it, while you learn
the repertoire of your opponent's wrist,
the repertoire which yours commands,
with every stroke surprising you,
as in a woman's glance the abundance,
secrecies, her body sports, in words
the glinting of her passion, stored away.

Those opposing roles, victor, victim
both, when they require re-enacting,
the moon as ever plays the luminous dome
above your god-and-man-scarred rock,
responsive to each nuance of the light
informing it with this, the latest scene.

The sweat you've shared between you,
juices drying on your hands and moonlit
belly, swirls out of the rutted, stain-
stiff sheets a fragrance stronger, more
anointing, than the myrrh, the frank-
incense the magi brought, a gleam
that would eclipse their beaten gold.

MAKING IT

(Jerusalem, July 4, 1980)

Easily as the moon
comes,
      as surprising . . .

      I
the eyes rising
to the shining surface
of this violin
        that you
have rented, full-
shouldered,
      the wood
old yet fragrant to the
nose, the finger,

its body a big, curving
sound . . .

      II
      and the stone
of this city, ages ground
in ages,
      the unblemished
sunlight daylong trooping
days
      sunk into it,

but pink & yellow flowers
welling out of it,
crowns in little like

the moon over it now,
as though newly polished,
newly made . . .

      III
make it new,
make it now,
make it . . .

IV
                the scrawny
young black cat, that
fixed us
                through a window
of our room with her
triangular
                Egyptian stare,
for all the skittish,
half mad,
                little kittens
already several times
a mother,

V
                crouches in the
doorway, shadow-silent,
waiting
                for the geckos,
prehistoric mini-monsters,
scarabs of good luck,

which, once dusk arrives,
out hunting, skitter
over
                our outdoor wall,
the chittering their name,
one with the voices
                                laden
in the air, expectant,
here in Israel . . .

VI
only appetite, that cat's,
the geckos', ancient
as the moon,
                its latest
luster that predates those
hoary rocks,
                like you and me,
the old gods throbbing
in us,

                  the looks flocked
from your fingers, penetrant
as any star,
                  only the song,
risen like a well-spring
from this violin,
                            out
of the prayers, the bloody
sighs, the wailing,
                            easily
      as the moon comes,
      its luminous calm, ever

            making it new,
            making it now,
            making it . . .

THE DEATH OF FATHERS

RUMMAGING inside yourself
for clues and coming up
with nothing more than old
familiar news, you think
you have it hard.
                    Your
father having died when you
were still a child, you keep,
it's true, but faded sense
of him.
            Nearly as bad,
not long after that
the village he was born
and lived in all his life
dispersed.
            And now, as if
it's joined, he with it,
the lost tribes of Virginia,
it survives, name only,
on discarded maps.
                    And you
blame blustering Pittsburgh,
the smoke of it, the noise
its days cannot contain,
the ruins it labors at.

But though my father died
when I was some years older,
I know, beyond all ordinary
disappearings, nothing
of his past, his country

(Hungary he called it,
a few oaths still peppery
on my tongue what's left
to prove it), least of all
his town.
            New vandals
rampant, kicking boundaries
about, entire nations on
the run, as though their
lands were made of wind-

46

blown sand, how expect
to know? (Only then, Hitler
bringing my father's country
home to him, father and I
huddled
        by the radio,
did I get a bitter sense
of who my father might have
been and was and of his
world
        in a past much
overlaid.) Like you I try
to ferret out whatever hints
of him from the one source
still available—myself.

Recall a few of his
loved saws like "The apple
falls not far from its tree."
But only a worm sticks
its fat tongue out at me.

Or "Teddy, I understand
you all right. Are you not
my son?" Well, was he not
my father? Clues or not,
I plunge into my writing,

chase fast scribbled
line on line, lean hard
on his robustious love:
his skill with animals:
his pleasure in the violin

he played by ear, gypsy
gaiety, abandon, gathered
up like grapes ripening
within his fingers' will:
his passion for his work,

my awe at watching him
delight in old things, new,
he bought to sell, green
filing cabinets he danced
among, as he, a boy then,

shoes astride his neck,
had skipped along (he told
me this?) the speckled path
dividing the Black Forest:
pride that almost drove

him, raging, over cliffs
and finally, when he would,
despite strong warnings,
mount a frisky horse, rode
him off forever,
              I there
as he stumbles up, eyes
closed, face set, the iron
bar lying just behind him
for what it's done
                  moved
little farther than before,
a last cry, mother's name,
still hot upon his lips.
He staggered about,

I, gripping his arm,
summon all my strength
("Am I not your son?"
Surely I can reach him,
haul him back) to learn—

as I shout "Father!"
over the growing chasm,
his breath slammed shut,
a wall instantly gone up—
the lesson never learned.

A COLLABORATION

A TINY FLY, attracted
to this letter I am writing—
does it, echoing this spring day
puffed through
        the window
as if out to find me, exhale
some nectared stuff?—lights on
a crooked twig
        of a word
and, like our old cat Hoppy,
briskly scrubbing its face, blots
the line:
        drinking, thinks
about it in ways I never thought
as it cuts short my thought
as well.
        So drinking, does
it gain the moment's nourishment
it needs to charter out new
heights?
        Has it flown here
on an errand of mercy, to save me
from a course I'd be absurd
to take?
        Whatever it's done,
a shortcut to meaning, tangles up
into opacities I never can
unravel.
        Call it a gadfly,
scoring my letter before it dries
and thereby taking it beyond
itself.
        Maybe unwittingly
assuring me that such, howsoever
I have wrought, is the end
it must come to.
        O well,
at least for the moment life
outside, high-flown life at that,
and I collaborate
        to make

a sign simple for those can read,
sign needing no meaning past
its shape upon the page.

As the fly has had a foot
in what I've done, so I have left
my mark on it; branded, fly
shows it
        wherever it goes.
Intentions apart, we can say
the fly, by interrupting so, has
happily inspired me.

SOUND

HOW PLEASING—remarkable
as well—that words like sound
and sound should be the same.

That now and then something's
name and the thing itself
precisely fit.
       We fumble
through ourselves in our lust
for one thing
       we can hold
to, baffled to know the stout-
hearted man
       we had loved
had disappeared like any word,
attenuated
       into drifting
air. O where and what, beyond
the moth, the rust,
       that
one touchstone we might trust?
And there,
       upon the darkening
day, burst from its steady
tide, a trill
       swells forth,
echoing while it reverberates
against, so sounds,
       each leaf:
a bird performing its brief
rite before the dark
       comes
on, and sleep. So sound alone
in its countless
       iteration
lasts, the urgent words struck
off and waiting
       to be recalled
of him cleft from our lives
who stormed them once
       with
anger as with deep resoundings
out of joy.

THE HOSTAGE

THE YOUNG MAN, all mixed up,
long before he used it dumped
his life to take on something
else because it sounded, if not
better, different.

              So he landed
in jail for assorted crimes,
in a country he couldn't name,
with little more than a pail
to remind him

              what his days
were coming to, and a straw cot
so hard, so narrow, it failed
to bear him and his dreams
which anyway grew

              so fat
that they, his sleep unable
to accommodate the least of them,
the cell too small, promptly
overran his days,

              until a fly
flew in and, lounging back,
seemed to ponder him.

              Returning,
pondered day by day.

              And sleep
began to work: the fly, at first
with wings and then without,
then wings, free of the body,
always bigger

              as they flapped,
flew—cell shaking like a storm-
struck ship—him out into the open
air beyond the need of wings
until he woke.

              Whatever fly
smuggled in of plums, lips, space
it hummed around, and yet denied
to sit and ponder him,

              grown fond
of it, he, catching it, tore off

its wings to keep it, not much
worse off then he.
            Appreciation,
which made his loneliness less,
made this possible.
            Between them,
needing little, they managed
a world. What's more, he could
afford to feed it fabulously.

LOOKING BACK

LOOK FOR an explanation?
You had reposed such trust
in everything you touched
that, touched in turn, hands
earned again and again, you
did not know how much each had
become a part of you:
                  your pot
which heated soup, the wine-
filled jars, that artful plate
that kept the sun, and faces too
bent over into it, the shining
waters of, as into joyous prayer,
under them
            the wobbling table
where you spread your hunger
with your talk, laughter trail-
ing after as you went to bed.

That shimmer, was it figures
flamed in dancing, seraph, star,
the streaming of your love?

And then you were expected
to let go without a glance!
Could they think you so
unfeeling, so unthankful?

Most of all to Him Who made
these things, long golden days

heaping the fields, your window
steepened by gold-bulging birds
and fruit.
            Or was it figures
flamed in dancing, seraph, star,
the glancing of His love?

Each thing dear in itself
as in the countless touches
shared with husband, children,
friends, your cat.
            So when,
that impulse sweeping over you,
you turned, the tears that might
have drowned your eyes lumped
into one.
            Should you not weep
for those denied a time to weep,
your household, the whole town,
lively once with all its evening
candle lights, that last time
sparkling—fire let loose, brim-
stone, cries a single crackling—
in your glance?

ULTRAMARINE

IT'S NOT so much
the rowdy water-colors of a pool,
my dear, wash over me whenever
I, schooled as I am in it,
regard your look,
                    but those
absorbed by you aeons before I
came to study, shadows lingering
of suave events, their actors,
furry, noble,
                    bent to drink.
These fervid scenes give forth
an opalescent privacy. And still
of power to suffuse a scent,
a husky music
                    keyed exactly
to your pace. But how mercurial
it is, the weather, in your look:
a morning's movement; winter
in a Russian mood;
                    the musk
of lowlands, silence soaking
up a forest dusk, intensified
by crows, now blazoning bronze
rumors of war.
                    Those rites
a sibyl tends are what you are
possessed by while I gawk at all
the many pictures moving far
beyond my depth.
                    Especially
when a tempest spurs them. Still
I gladly plunge into this surf,
reflections strewing round—
flakes in a swirl
                    and edges
like the cataract a cloudburst
fattens—faster than their first
occasion for the feeling you
afford them:
                    gladly cast myself,
the breakers riding me, aside.

WORD FOR WORD

EACH PHRASE, at me overwhelmingly,
word for word makes conspicuous sense.
But when I think, my mind intense,
to grasp the whole,
                        the world
behind reverberates, a monstrous
smithy, fashioning—the lightning
and the thunder one—sheet-metal-
shuddering dew.
                        Have you, sped
to outlandish places, furbished up
your speech, so verified your reveries,
that now the scene itself—
                        the one
you plucked like any cuckoo to compose
your echoing, well-plaited spell—
speaks through:
                        a world I've glimpsed
in dreams, in passion, those unique
occasions when the self, no longer
clogged, enjoys itself as though
it hardly is?
                        Or does this world
root still, but your words (mine as
well) have lit on it at such an angle,
the way some strong-willed mirrors
work,
                I cannot get my bearings,
and objects I assumed I know turn
sides to me cacophonous yet alluring
in their novelty?
                        Let's say they are,
these notes, receipted bills for goods
you, carefully uncovering, bring home
to sort in taking schemes dictated
by your private need.
                        Anyone can see
the shimmer on them of a stranger moon,
sheens too from arcane rituals, cold,
bewildering, in their lucidity.

DOUBLE TALK

THIS LANGUAGE bids you
utter things, at times unwittingly
and far below the level—early spring
invisibly at work in buds, a seed,
greedy wren eggs—of hearing.

You feel stubborn, put upon,
an awkward foreigner. So you struggle
to resist its countless innuendoes,
easy air of wit and knowingness,
that mien of flouncing by

here many times before.
But then you wonder whether, by
struggling so, you have not played
into its hands. Prodded, have you not
responded to the whispering

behind a woman's voice,
a child's, apparently less than
ghost, yet splendidly inspiriting this
flesh? As to the rush of wind-sped
rain so cool, else to the

summer breeze so hot,
upon the skin. A wily language
beneath language which you wish to net
within your own. So both of you
willy-nilly change a little:

admitting you, making
concessions, phrases now must
learn to live in your pronouncings
and your waywardnesses, something more
than mere syntactic tangle.

Such befalls words moved
into another language, befalls
language so invaded, yet assimilating.
And when, like two defiant bloods,
your interests collide,

one heart the riverbed,
at flood you root in one another.
Who'd have predicted your differences,
as they resoundingly fuse you two,
make each one more itself.

THE READINGS

NOT THAT smudgy moon—
and not, their beams having
long ago forsaken them, the pin-
prick stars—elusive like some
revery, a scruff of mist left
over, puffball in the grass-
green dawn, dew wading,

  but the stalky
irises, white among yellow,
whites with purple streakings,
like the lids of dreaming girls,
whose limbs and manes Greek fire
kindled, Sappho's lissome
thoroughbreds.
    Siberian
you call them. But, unfurled
on morning's scroll, for exact
and delicate markings they look
Japanese.
    Clusters also
by, each one a stiff bouquet,
of rhododendrons, deeply bitten,
crumpled, leaf-brown, February
having seared them, neighbor
azaleas, already ghost-lit
orange.
   Such the spheres I play
astronomer to:
     mahogany-glossy
as he is, still strong in hunger,
clamorous like insistent crows
his predawn cry, our nether star
humped Hoppy, kitchen hugging,
sleep-possessed,

and you, body
candid against the sheets, glow
these lowly, little planets glide
in tune to and I read by, read
the till now hidden meanings,
so absorbing I, puffball sunken,
read no more.

A WALK IN THE PARK

THOUGH IT MAY have changed a little
to remain the same, it is in no way over,
that scrap from the remote past. Like
a pebble for fingering lodged in
your pocket.
             Popped to the surface
now, the stroll in the Luxembourg Gardens,
dressed in the day's snow-trimmed attitude,
you took again and again many years ago—

winter relishing its uniform wealth,
like Eskimos those fur-wrapped children,
shrieks, delighted, shoving sailboats
off—
        ambling through, stands altogether
by you, with the flailing Punch and Judy
show. But though its jumping patrons cheer,
a shadow (is it here or from that day?)
fretting the bleak light,
                a few leaves
clattered to the gusts nagging at them,
the chestnuts barely shrug. As if, caught
mid-act, the statues, pallid, freeze.
Still whatever's happened
               since then,
in you but also in the Gardens, practices
its most accommodating tact. Like that
artist's imperceptibly growing blindness,
brushed into huge water-lilies lolled
across the pond.
          And that particular stroll
(some other?), sly enough not to attract
too much attention, tugs your sleeve,

the latest beggars
             more than offspring
as they greet you with the original hunger,
moments brisk if mostly for the vigor
of their recollection.
             The casual way
it starts again assures you that your walk,
proceeding inside time, exceeds that time,
as it predicts, since making possible,
each new act you may encounter.

COMING ATTRACTIONS

YOU KNOW to take directions
from the rain. It is a telling
landmark.
             In their rainbow-throat-
swelled cooing pouter-pigeons
also cue.
             And any fire you
may crouch by instantly exposes
landscape to the core,
             the spirit
all things else would flesh,
a ghost thereafter.
             Do not try
to cling to what you are: at once
it changes.
             Rest assured steady
drifting is good will enough
to mollify a sea.
             This field
too, leaned on its elbow, a straw
stuck in its mouth
             as it enjoys
its weed work, bees wreathed
round its head,
             takes you,
trying it on with every sense,
wherever you want to go.
             Standing
here, a lamp for someone else,
you rout up a mouse

              or two;
from ruffling wings crows shake
out crackled dark
             that trees grow
dense. Yet when the evening,
till now stored,
            one multi-
pleated screen, inside the light,
unfolds,
           the moon bursts forth,
the guttering lamp of some
body else,
         body else of her,
the sky, the future, in her look.
By lights like these
           how choice
your errors, all crumbling
things.
        An impulse, brooding
in the air, readies its surprises.

VARIATIONS ON A FAVORITE THEME

Early One Morning

EARTH'S PLENTY in a little room?
Call to mind a painting, Chardin,
Vermeer, opulent for being
simple,
      its pots and pans
keeping the outer world at bay,
pictures, maps, lovingly arrayed,
composing themselves
              around
the woman who, the light focused,
weighs gems in a scale, bright
with her look.
         But the day
floods in, notably amassing scale
by scale, like a salmon hooked—
throughout
      its battering
upstream, the waters bracing-
cold and, flashed in the splatter,
a thrashing
        as if partner
of the leap—to its nativity.
Like you, practicing, practicing,
in a room:
       a lustrous bough,
your violin transmutes the beams
streamed through your window
mote on mote to melody
            that,
time and fate made light of, made
so much at home, we, knowing
we fail to understand,
          feel
light-hearted since we realize we
need not trouble: what we do
enough,
      that plenty heaped
meticulous as in a little shining
scale, the scale deft fingers
and your bow divine.

Outside It's Tuesday

AS THOUGH to turn every bit
of early morning air into its trill,
over and over and over, then over
again, a bird perched in our maple
is repeating its four-tone row.

So you, first testing the strings
against your ear—one after another
you pluck them, press—start
practicing.
        A thrum established,
presto, the airy earth of it arises:
thick as crickets' ceaseless hum,
as hornets, in lush summer grasses,
listening and loosing voices
while they listen,
                  creatures spring
full-blown to your fingers, ready
to hail in whatever you require.
Fed on skills your hands excel in,
instantly it's here, that passage:

farms and arbors deeply breathing
fragrances they, breathing, deepen;
towns abuzz with their inhabitants,
rapt in their works and days,
                      traffic
crackling away like field artillery
and distant, echoing, great guns,
the din a steady network underscored
by uttermost silence an abyss reports.

Staked in that open plot which you,
your violin, and these notes conspire,
all look to you, to music.
                Through
your strings the world, more spacious
as it turns upon itself, is passing,
our maple riding its dappled tide.

MAINSTAY

for Hoppy
on his twentieth birthday

I

YOU, Hoppy, crept out
on the backporch, flopping
to its shag-rug, your sleep,
age- and August-drugged,
still burdening—
                    the look
        on you like Socrates
        just after the Symposium,

        gruff Picasso his maid
        and mistress each day had
        to drag out from his bed,

        but most of all
        that old Jew, his last
        gasp begging, "Please be
        so kind, a glass tea"—

how much can I expect
of you?
            More than ever
you suffer my affection,
even when it rouses
as it does right now
into gusts of roughhouse.
For you know me well
enough to know it ends
in purring hugs, in food.

II

And yet, a front tooth
gone, one nicked ear slack,
your leftpaw whiskers bitten
off, I putting you down,
you totter
            over images
too swift, too vague—many
a mouse and bird once stalked,

64

the chipmunks, chattering—
to keep, all your nine lives
sadly huddled side by side
beside you.
                    No wonder
any dream that I might press
on you to share, any high-
falutin fear, you disregard,

> as would that aged Jew,
> Picasso bent to his final
> escapade, or Socrates
> set on the last debate.

III

Yet here you are, gazing
up at me with sharply
calculating eyes, gold-
amber still, the appetite
behind, its very gnawing
strength, a last resort,

> to some degree a mainstay.

EARTHRISE

LIKE the conquistadors
our moon men lusted after novelty,
world out of this world no one
had ever visited before?

Every second passing,
though it seem a commonplace,
pries an unexpected door. Every
second a stepping into the unknown,

a leaping in the mind
that the breath catches, the heart
in its sputtering flame matches
against the delicious fear.

Moon more than enough
this body, this pocked earth
we wander, space enough the heaven
our looks dart through,

our talk: earth flies
with us, swamps and mountains,
eagles peaking, snow-packed clouds,
the rivers pouring over,

cataracts. And burrowed
far below, those furry meteors
of the mineral dark: mole sedulous
with sidekick squeaky bat

and mouse. Those also,
bearded comets, sparks struck
off, fellow travelers streaming by,
like us equipped to people

briefly our atmosphere.
Last night the fireflies composed
a galaxy, a complex universe,
among the trees. Falling

together mouth to mouth,
the dark, its planets, backing us,
we sighed forth air unhusked
a god might yearn to use.

The moon on our hands
and everywhere, space fell
away. For the rapture whirling us
a song too close to hear.

EVERY SECOND THOUGHT

And thence return me to my Milan, where
Every third thought shall be my grave.
> —Prospero

I

A GREY and dampish thing
this day, here in the winter
of your years, each blustering
winter all year long.
                    Airs
muttered round your ears,
you huddle by your fitful fire.
Light, just enough
                    for dark
to score itself, a riches else
too packed to be spelled out,
selects medleying scenes:

the trees one ruddy gold
and green their leaves, blow-
ing forth a roundelay, repeated
by trill-volleying birds.

Scenes also, riding flames,
make you forget this dusty spot,
scapes in which the sky shot
fire-caps
                    bridling the sea,
the world a hovering loveliness.
Still, shivering, do you not
regret their loss,
                    those powers
that could snare the world,
from urchins to the elements,
into one
                    comprehensive song?
In your regardless corner-shade
you drowse: the hours pass
remarkable
                    as drifter clouds.
Yet clouds, building at a glance,

once cobbled sky a causeway
nymphs and deities
                        employed.
Who pauses near, amazed to think
this frayed grey stalk young
crowned itself
                        with flowers?

II

Not she, the flower crowning all
the rest, one time your all
in all.
          Vast miles on miles
and many hardships piled between,
answering calls more urgent
than your sighing,
                        she has
fled with her husband the prince
and their children for his
plotting uncle
                        who ousted
the prince's father. And not
your brother, villain sufficient
earlier, snake-wise
                        lurked
upon your age to stir rebellion
and, with help from Naples,
to ensure
                        your present, last
forsakenness. Though your people
venerate you still, had you
not proved
                        passive as before
(how he must have scoffed at you
assuming you could do without
your scepter
                        of a wand, trim
magic. Tell how much they served
that first treacherous time!
Could you,
                        adrift in a leaky
boat with Miranda and your brave
devices, bid the wind behave?
Even later,

when your mastery
was complete, the spirits called
at will, what power could
you exercise
                        past that isle,
what skill to conjure up voyages
would fly you safely home?),
he would have had
                                you killed.
Or once more cast out on the sea.

                        III
Your distant island, however
forsaken,
                        was never like this!
Yet already there at best you knew
the play you put on moved none
but those responsive.
                        Others,
stony at your music, obedient only
to their own desires, must go
the way
                        that they were going.
Still even here, a rustle heard,
flambeaus, much like leafy morning,
blossom
                        to awaken scattered
corners of your day; dense forests
stretching, out of the shadows
one after one
                        shapes emerge,
as a fragrance or a comely cry
each richly prinked in your senses.
Women are they,
                        supple nymphs
flourished by like the overlapping
leaves and puffy flowers, pink
for the musk they shed,
                                with lords
in their gaudy plumage peacocks
yoked to a goddess' chariot?
See!—

IV

your dreaming, fired,
nods?—a hag, blue-lidded, ridden
after the goddess, ruffians
wrangling.
                    Murmurs sharpen.
Out of air—old age wields its
own charm!—familiar echoes speak
to you.
                "Had you an inkling
then, you, drowned in words, what
thing of shame gnawing away
a younger brother is?
                            Always
to follow at fixed distance foot-
prints casting dust into his
face.
            And yet I was expected
to stand humbly, yes, abjectly by
while you, ignoring me as you
ignored the state,
                        let it go,
the poverty which ate the people,
corruption honeycombing all,
to play,
            man though you were,
with toys, till I took over. War
then which I alone knew how to use,
and how to quell,
                        restoring
welfare, a busy peace. Perhaps,
in aging helpless, younger than I,
you understand."

V

The features
change. A snarling grates. Inside
it brushes crackling, squawks,
yaps, chittering.
                    "Me, your slave,
first plucked, lowly, rooted
thing, from out my place,
you, finding filthy,
                            threw

71

back again. An earth you may have
thought me, not better than
the badgers.
                    Far, far below
your spirits. Yet more than them
you needed me. Without the berries
and fish I brought
                    how long
would you have lived, so reared
your spells? Without the logs I
lugged try conjuring your scenes!"

                    VI
More motley flutters by.
Resembles beings you imagined
you commanded. Unruly as the stuff
you wrenched them from,
                                        are
they grown fractious at your sighs?
Actors of a traveling company,
their fleering antics,
                          tumbles,
mimic you, your tale, your monster.
A wretched copy of an English
writer's work,
                    said to possess
some gift but neither burdened nor
embarrassed by truth, a light-
weight drama,
             full of tricks,
put on years ago about your trials
on the island. At this late day
nothing left but horseplay.

Caliban, a tawdry sideshow,
languishes far off in Naples?
Or did we, fierce to leave, forget
him,
        the world of the island
closing round, once more a vine-
entangled, branch-sequestered nook?
That poem you read—
                    had it

already been composed?—called
something like "Caliban Remembers,"
took it quite for granted
                    he
had stayed behind and, able of much
more than ever you suspected,
did amazing things.

VII
                Startled
(waking is it in a frenzied dream?),
you feel the battering, gross,
exultant heart,
                now too much
for you, of that lush isle attuned
to full-blown tempests your hand
could control.
                    Puppets it swept by,
gods, nereids, the burly sea
but mimicry, its combers
a fulfilling
            of your will,
then brought to heel that grunting
breath and stinking body, bent
on being nothing
                but itself.

VIII
The stinking, unannounced, begins
again. Even as you rummage
tattered books,
                half hoping
you will stumble on old, powerful
words, like dolphins leaped
from weeks-long,
                somber waves,
or in a thicket thyme fermenting,
rhapsodies. That moonshine
heaping the page,
                the fire's
lambencies, its shadow shuddered
for a moth flown by, first
loitering

as on the twiglet
your sigh extends, can they once
more highlight the phrases,
fix them
in a murmurous glow?
Or do the letters, twisting, rise,
ant-like bearing fluttered,
nacreous things
many times
their size, to publish astounding
news?

IX
Lichens you came on,
weather stains,
each wing and
petal unfurling an intricate callig-
raphy, were they not printer
ink to you?
Maps instant on
their treasures like that writing—
treasures radiant everywhere
it touches—
of spring rain.
Facsimiles, blooming on the rocks,
in look as in their fragrance
Arabic.
Out of taut strings'
clangor sudden gales and mermaids
singing. But now you realize
the clay, clumped
under all,
sped you on to nothing other than
this prosaic world you dreamt
a word could alter.

X
Still
you pick up sticks, the withy you
peel now, mumbling, brandish
in the air,
as though it
can, wand-like, flick wonders out.

Just so that chair, your eyes
fixed on it,
          by firelight
one moment bulked in gleams
(as if, hands out, Miranda, young,
smiling, sits there;
                    then,
with you about to speak to her,
her mother, your delicate Cecilia,
a birth her death,
                 whom you
had neglected even in her illness
for your studies; and you set
on embracing her,
                she turns
into a harpy: "Me you can embrace
never more than you did then.
Shade I was, shade am!").

And so it dims, the chair.
Or was it that ring she gave you,
through the years preserved?
Rubbed, as now,
                owns power
more than your magic works, works
on you to rouse this feeling,
power overwhelming
                    you denied,
the whole world harsh against you,
earth a grave. The withy works
no tittle better
                than your mind
trying to recall that sodden
book, lost in the breaker-
ridden past.
            At least one
potent formula you seem to hear
faint whispers of: "Next be
the wind design . . . ,"
                        the flaw
of your poor, porous memory
that blows the rest away.
Blows whiffs of him

rough to
your nostrils as from the fetid
recess of a cave (or maybe
your own slow decay?),

              reek
you felt—air crammed with it
smutching everything—you never
would forget.

XI

        The wind high
in the masts, time fast arrived
to board the ship. He, cowed
by sailor jeers,

           the dashing
waves, and what would lie ahead,
hid himself within a covert
only he could know.

                 Lives he
still? And still, sprawled back
beneath a bee-spun canopy
of woodbine,

         sunk in dreams
of the heavens opening to shower
on him ceaseless bounty,
forms danced

            round his head,
midges pied in a hum, remembers
you? Alone there now, like
you alone,

         and all, Miranda,
you, the rest, chimerae, masques,
mere slurring husks of air?
Bites

     bring him back, stray
words still bitter to his tongue?
Remembers you, tyrannical,
would have subdued

           his will,
that wayward and free-flowing
like the isle's luxuriant growth,
to yours?

       Your book he must

have fished, its arts still live.
Else why feel heart-strings
tugged,
       a twanging winged
through you?

XII
       "However we began,
no springs you found in the likes
of me.
       Speech you taught me
that for a time I loved—so loved
you all the more—the world
thus singled out.
       I, words
guiding, eyes skyward, with words
the stars flock-like startled
in their place
       and uttered
perfect, round as the O of my
mouth, honey-golden droplet in my
mouth, the moon,
       the sun,
you, and most of all, frisking in
and out the rest—much like
a river sparkling
       as it rides
the crest it pushes forth—Miranda.
All flowering star-like in
their grassy bed.
       Not least
among you me. But words you could
never know I, need prodding,
ferreted out,
       scampering in
coverts, marmosets, young scamels.
This until words, crusting,
became a curse,
       a way of worsting
things, hobbling and stying,
like Ariel in that trunk.
Thereon I saw
       that things,

as if ashamed, behind those names
recoiling, more than ever hid.
Hid you did too.
                    Sky-walker
you would be, what past your magic
and yourself could you admit?
Thine and mine
                    you harped on,
mine by more you claimed for thine,
me midst an endless wrangling.
Oh you had freed
                    a spirit
from its tree, airy one my dam
trussed there, but nothing of that
tree itself, the self in me."

                    XIII
You had planned to use him
kindly, and you did; had planned
to set him—when he learned
the many lessons
                    to become
a man, his reasoning upright—
free. Man proper he was that day,
upright, rearing!
                    Air you
might curb, never flesh and blood . . .
a something in that moment
(was it Ariel?)
                    warned you.
Panicked, you rushed to the place.
There they lay, she, eyes
shut, clothes torn,
                    and he
over her, breathless, hands water-
bugs darting upon her body;
bending,
                    pursed lips to hers.
Furious, gripping a branch, again
and again you strike. Strength
matching your fury,
                    dead
he must have been. Up, blood

on him, rage, he yanks the branch
from you,
        raises it, holds,
then, breaking it, bundles off.
Later: "Saw her, butterfly chased,
plunge into that pit.
                 I—
not you, your magic—clambered
down, hauled her out. Her fainted
I, trying to waken,
             find no
more a child. Manhood must assert
itself. Love lost, between us
nothing but hot snarling."

XIV

And if he told the truth?
Whatever the story came to, shaky
truce was the most that you
could hope for.
        Then how,
especially on such tiny island
with no one near to oversee, free
him?
        (Not like that one
who, teetered on dawn's dewy
ledge, quarries whatever music he
desires from a cloud
           and,
nature all engrossing, impervious
to any print, has no designs
on you.)
        And so, back turned
to the day, crouching over black-
and-white, those bees dried
out,
      you taught him nothing
better than hostility, who might
have taught you—did you once
acknowledge
           his sufficiency,
the way the wild isle fit him
like a rippling skin?—ripeness

in that isle:
                    what things
he saw, what things he knew, had
to, to survive: the private
lives
          of beetle, otter, bat,
shifty moods of day and night,
hoopoe just at perching rainbows,
jubilant,
               looping through
their flights, to conjoin and
multiply their hues. Meantime you,
the world
               waiting on you,
played Narcissus never better
served, gaping in a stagnant pond.
The isle abounded.

                    XV
                    Jutting
through those multi-colored cries
of name-defying birds, bare
rock you judged it,
                    a sea-
like, leaped, and leaping lizard
green, eager to engulf you,
your child,
               those precious books,
the dream you clung to. Rock
jut also here in rotting,
pullulating Milan.
                    You could
not sense that isle might satisfy,
as it exceeded, any dream.
Even the flame
                    insinuating
through those words you followed
like a rutted highway, quick
with lightsome traffic,
                    elfin
images, set off in gold, in song.
Inside these stone-cold walls
dreaming the little
                    you have

left, at moments briefly you can
muster it. This fire blazing
does its part,
                many a mutter
hived as in a secret, moss-bound
cleft of memory, scents too,
you scarcely noticed.

XVI
                Now emerge:
your body, twinging, has begun
again. So it occupies you
with a lore—
                pangs, swarmed
inside and out, as of fiend imps
perfecting their technique
along your spine,
                prick you
like porcupines aroused; and you,
at last step-child to him
you could not father,
                bear
his every ache—you, worlds ago,
dismissed. No feather, leaf,
or fragrance left?
                Everlast-
ingly you wear that rasping reek
of him, stink your own decay
revives.
                Could he but know
he might—what you most wish—
finally forgive. Those two, body,
breath, sweet music
                out of
tumult, tumult once more claims
to sound its always growing
triumph.
                Till its impulse,
strident through your breathing—
so it was before: the storm
you made,
                the sky on fire
crashing into the sea, made you—
work to free you, as the body

81

withers into air.
                    To him,
the all-embracing, you surrender,
of a love that never needs
to know of love.

1 12/93

Andrew Keenan-Bolger
& Kate Wetherhead

WITHDRAWN

Jack &
Louisa

Act 3

PENGUIN WORKSHOP
An Imprint of Penguin Random House

PENGUIN WORKSHOP

Penguin Young Readers Group

An Imprint of Penguin Random House LLC

Text copyright © 2017 by Andrew Keenan-Bolger and Kate Wetherhead.
Illustrations copyright © 2017 by Ben Kirchner. All rights reserved.
Previously published in hardcover in 2017 by Grosset & Dunlap.
This paperback edition published in 2018 by Penguin Workshop,
an imprint of Penguin Random House LLC, 345 Hudson Street,
New York, New York 10014. PENGUIN and PENGUIN WORKSHOP
are trademarks of Penguin Books Ltd, and the W colophon is
a trademark of Penguin Random House LLC. Printed in the USA.

Cover illustrations by Ben Kirchner

Library of Congress Control Number: 2017932715

ISBN 9781524784973   10 9 8 7 6 5 4 3 2 1